A CRITIQUE OF
JEAN-PAUL SARTRE'S ONTOLOGY

THE UNIVERSITY OF NEBRASKA

A CRITIQUE OF
JEAN-PAUL SARTRE'S ONTOLOGY

MAURICE NATANSON

HASKELL HOUSE PUBLISHERS LTD.
Publishers of Scarce Scholarly Books
NEW YORK. N. Y. 10012
1972

HASKELL HOUSE PUBLISHERS Ltd.

Publishers of Scarce Scholarly Books

280 LAFAYETTE STREET

NEW YORK. N. Y. 10012

Library of Congress Cataloging in Publication Data

Natanson, Maurice Alexander, 1924-
   A critique of Jean-Paul Sartre's ontology.

   Reprint of the 1951 ed., which was issued as no. 6 of
University of Nebraska studies, new ser.
   Bibliography: p.
   1. Sartre, Jean Paul, 1905-   --Ontology.
2. Existentialism. I. Title. II. Series: Nebraska.
University. University of Nebraska studies, new ser.,
no. 6.
B2430.S34N25 1972   111   72-8367
ISBN 0-8383-1412-0

Printed in the United States of America

CONTENTS

Part II

EVALUATION

FOR
CHARLES AND KATE
LOIS AND CHARLES

ACKNOWLEDGMENT

A number of persons have directly or indirectly aided me in achieving a greater degree of philosophic comprehension as well as in completing this work. The expression of my thanks to them is more than a formality.

I am indebted to Drs. Bouwsma, Patterson, Storer, and Waters—members of the Department of Philosophy of the University of Nebraska, 1948–1950.

Mr. John Chapman of the University Library has skillfully assuaged my bibliographical pains.

Dr. Boyd G. Carter of the University Department of Modern Languages has helped me with my numerous language problems.

Miss Emily Schossberger, Editor of the University of Nebraska Press, has aided me considerably in preparing my manuscript for publication.

Any note of thanks for the aid my wife, Lois Natanson, has given me would be inadequate for the expression of my appreciation.

I am happy, finally, to state my thanks and gratitude to Professor W. H. Werkmeister, who has devoted a great deal of his time to bringing this work to its most successful form, and whose persistent interest in my philosophic advancement and welfare has meant much to me.

INTRODUCTION[1]

"Why is my pain perpetual,
and my wound incurable,
which refuseth to be healed?"
—Jeremiah

"Existentialism" today refers to faddism, decadentism, morbidity, the "philosophy of the graveyard"; to words like fear, dread, anxiety, anguish, suffering, aloneness, death; to novelists such as Jean–Paul Sartre, Dostoievski, Camus, Kafka; to philosophers like Kierkegaard, Heidegger, Marcel, Jaspers, and Sartre—and because it refers to, and is concerned with, all of these ideas and persons, existentialism has lost any clearer meaning it may have originally possessed. Because it has so many definitions, it can no longer be defined. As Sartre writes:

> "Most people who use the word existentialism would be embarrased if they had to explain it, since, now that the word is all the rage, even the work of a musician or painter is being called existentialist. A gossip columnist . . . signs himself *The Existentialist,* so that by this time the word has been so stretched and has taken on so broad a meaning, that it no longer means anything at all." [2]

This state of definitional confusion is not an accidental or negligible matter. An attempt will be made in this introduction to account for the confusion and to show why any definition of existentialism involves us in a tangle. First, however, it is necessary to state in a tentative and very general manner what points of view are here intended when reference is made to existentialism.

Sartre means by existentialism the doctrine "that existence precedes essence, or, if you prefer, that subjectivity must be the starting point." [3] We must begin with subjectivity, not simply because it is

---

[1] With minor changes this introduction appeared in the Winter, 1950, issue of *The University of Kansas City Review.*

[2] Sartre, J–P., *Existentialism,* 14–15.

[3] *Ibid.,* 15.

1

some sort of convenient starting point but because man has become problematic to himself, and self-consciously so. His problem is his own existence. The traditional categories of cognition are not only insufficient for a solution but are utterly inapplicable, for the problem is not one of cognition, certainly not one of cognition in the ordinary sense of the term.

Nietzsche exclaimed: "God is dead," and men are faced with the profound responsibility of deciding for themselves, choosing for themselves, acting for themselves, and being *themselves;* i.e., choosing authentic existence rather than "losing" themselves in the crowd, becoming a "non-entity," escaping reality. In this transvaluation of all values more is at stake than traditional Christianity. According to tradition a man could not only be saved but he could depend upon the state, count on his family, and similar institutions. The crisis of our age, however, of which the existentialist writers speak is the loss of faith in the absoluteness of Reason, of Science, and of Logic. Ours is the time of a-logicality. Man is burning between chance and despair, between hope and nothingness, between salvation and guilt.

Existentialism emerges as deeply felt concern with and for the concrete reality of the individual: it is his existence that is vital, and it is he who must define himself. It is no longer possible to lose oneself in the System or hope to reveal existence by analytic procedures used in the investigation of "life" or the "cosmos." The individual as such, in his unique subjectivity, in his personal existence, is at stake; and existentialism holds that the essence of a person may not be revealed by reference to an *a priori* theory of man or any religious interpretation that speaks of man prior to and apart from his actual existence.

In view of this tentative definition of our subject matter, it is reasonable to ask about the history of this idea or complex of ideas referred to as existentialism; whether it represents a movement which has deep roots in the history of philosophy, or whether it began as a literary interest. It is possible to speak, if we wish, of an existential "attitude" and trace the origins of this attitude in past cultures. However, since the purpose of this work is not historical, the "tracings" that will be done will be rather casual and incomplete. We shall review the history and background of existentialism merely in an attempt to find a more adequate definition and to assign to it more properly its place in the general history of ideas.

However, we are faced at once with a specific difficulty; for it is obvious that in some sense every philosopher, every man who has ever "philosophized," has been concerned with the problem of man's existence. It soon becomes meaningless, therefore, to search for historical antecedents of existentialism unless we restrict the meaning of the term "existentialist" to those philosophers or thinkers whose specific concern is the concrete subjectivity of man as it defines his actual and concrete existence. And even with this restriction of the term some names will have to be considered whose bearers are at best but doubtful "existentialists." [4]

The reaction of Socrates against the Sophists was more than a rejection of rhetoric and fee-taking; it was the turning to a deeper respect for the problems of men. These problems concerning the Good Life, Justice, and so on were not simply artificial debates in which the victor was the "cleverer" who might take the opposite side the next day to exhibit his verbal dexterity. For Socrates, philosophy was a communion with persons, in the act of conversation recognizing their right to bring forth their ideas—to give birth to their potential idea-children. These ideas, again, are not the issues of mathematics or physics, but rather the great ethical and social problems. There is an ambiguous attitude toward reason and its products: an acceptance of the validity of the rational process and a denial of purely rational problems. It is thus possible through dialectic to reason our way to an understanding of the human situation, but it is at the same time more vital to discuss that human situation than work out equations or puzzles in geometry. Socrates, the life of Socrates, is an affirmation of the untechnical and human in philosophy, and we shall see a little later that it is largely for this reason that Kierkegaard is so "taken" by Socrates. He is the antithesis of the "professor" that Kierkegaard railed against. But to summarize: Socrates asks, what would you rather have, a geometer's argument or a myth? He gives us myths that have as their orientation-point man's place in the market-square, the language of "shoemakers" and "shepherds," the specificity of the human condition.

We face in subsequent philosophy the fluctuations in valuation of the worth, importance, and primacy of the individual. From Descartes

---

[4] For a historical study of existentialism see Kurt Hoffman, *Existential Philosophy: A Study of its Past and Present Forms.*

to Hegel we witness the decline of the centrality of the individual. If modern philosophy is roughly dated with the Cartesian philosophy, we may assert that until the period of the reactions against Descartes and Hegel which came with Pascal and Kierkegaard, the story of modern philosophy is the story of the loss of individuality, the languishing of existential subjectivity.

Descartes in his search for "clear and distinct" ideas ignored the immediate fact of human existence. The dualism of *res extensa* and *res cogitens* is founded essentially on a separation of man's essence from his existence, and Descartes never succeeded in welding the two together again, or in synthesizing them. The reaction of Pascal was to expose man as a feeling creature, a finite creature caught in the paradox of his search for the infinite, a creature that must believe his heart because his reason is inadequate. Consider some of Pascal's Pensées:

> "Let us then take our compass; we are something, and we are not everything. The nature of our existence hides from us the knowledge of first beginnings which are born of the Nothing; and the littleness of our being conceals from us the sight of the Infinite." [5]

> "This is our true state; this is what makes us incapable of certain knowledge and of absolute ignorance. We sail within a vast sphere, ever drifting in uncertainty, driven from end to end. When we think to attach ourselves to any point and to fasten to it, it wavers and leaves us; and if we follow it, it eludes our grasp, slips past us, and vanishes for ever. Nothing stays for us. This is our natural condition, and yet most contrary to our inclination; we burn with desire to find solid ground and an ultimate sure foundation whereon to build a tower reaching to the Infinite. But our whole groundwork cracks, and the earth opens to abysses." [6]

And, of course:

> "The heart has its reasons, which reason does not know." [7]

The brief protest of Pascal is swept up in the Hegelian Surge. The Hegelian System which promises everything, the All-inclusive System,

---

[5] Pascal, B., *Pensées*, 24–25.
[6] *Ibid.*, 25.
[7] *Ibid.*, 95.

makes of the Pascalian heart a determined point in the process. A dialectical mechanism is constructed by Hegel. The unfolding of the Absolute promises to reveal the slightest incident, but in revealing a particle, a tiny happening, a single heart, it collapses the blown uniqueness of the person. Inwardness of the personality, the felt life is ruptured by a plan that engulfs the past, present, and future of man. Kierkegaard is Hegel's punishment.

The positing of "the self against the System" [8] rests on the belief that speculation (by which Kierkegaard meant the Hegelian philosophy) never reaches the Self but falls short of it. The exploration of the Self is the burden of Kierkegaardian existentialism. By the Self Kierkegaard means the "inwardness" of the individual, that unique aspect of each of us which seeks to synthesize infinity and finitude, temporality and eternity, freedom and necessity. The Self faces the problem of salvation, of its "fear and trembling" and its despair. As a theistic existentialist, Kierkegaard is concerned "to find out where the misunderstanding lies between speculation and Christianity." [9] The traditional and orthodox Christianity of his time is unacceptable to him. The ritual and pomp of the church have led away from the essential Christian problem: the individual Self. But the issue is clear for Kierkegaard: how is the Self to discover itself, to define itself, to *found* itself? Kierkegaard speaks of stages in life's way which lead from the undiscovered to the founded Self.

The first stage he calls the Aesthetic. At this level the individual leads the life of the crowd. He loses himself in a bundle of activities. He investigates the sensuous and sensual life. He faces everyone but himself. The road from outwardness to inwardness crosses next the Ethical Stage. Shocked from the aesthetic life, the individual finds himself suddenly without props, and he reels from the knowledge that what he has hitherto experienced is vain and illusory. He feels his loneliness and recognizes his life as "sickness unto death." The third or Religious Stage involves man directly with the issue of his relation to God. He recognizes in his fear and trembling that it is only a blind "leap to faith" through which he can reach God. There is no rational guidance in this dialectic toward God. An incomprehensible divine grace is active in its operation.

[8] Grene, M., *Dreadful Freedom*. "The Self Against the System" is the partial title of Ch. 2.

[9] *Ibid.*, 15.

The dualisms of Kierkegaard are those of finite man seeking an infinite God, yielding the strange paradox of the God-man; the attempt of a finite and imperfect reason striving to comprehend the infinite and incomprehensible, giving rise to the paradox of thought trying to think the unthinkable; and man seeking to synthesize the incompatible elements of his own ethic and God's law, which is the paradox of faith. The Bible story of Abraham and Isaac is to Kierkegaard the desperate essence of man's condition. The story is described in Kierkegaard's *Fear and Trembling*. Abraham is desirous of following the law of the community, the law of his people. He loves his son, yet he is requested by God to sacrifice his son. He must transcend man's law and obey God's. Also, in Isaac alone exists Abraham's promise of the future. If he kills Isaac, he slays as well the possibility of new generations. Isaac is his delight and he must yet choose God. Kierkegaard asks:

> "Who gave strength to Abraham's arm? Who held his right hand up so that it did not fall limp at his side? He who gazes at this becomes paralyzed. Who gave strength to Abraham's soul, so that his eyes did not grow dim, so that he saw neither Isaac nor the ram? He who gazes at this becomes blind.—And yet rare enough perhaps is the man who becomes paralyzed and blind, still more one who worthily recounts what happened. We all know it—it was only a trial." [10]

The necessity of God is the reflection of man's guilt, of his finitude. Marjorie Grene writes:

> "Subjectivity can be truly subjective only in the confrontation of the individual with God, since only the absolute is completely indescribable beyond the inroads of abstraction and objectivity. Only before God is a man really himself, because it is only before God that he is finally and irretrievably alone. But before God the finite individual is as nothing; and it is the bitter realization of that nothingness that marks the religious stage of existence." [11]

The dialectic of Kierkegaard is integral to his philosophy. Here is the Self, but the Self in its contradictions and in its confusions and humors. Paradox is the booby-trap into which we plunge immediately upon reading Kierkegaard, just as Alice went down the rabbit hole. In

[10] Kierkegaard, S., *Fear and Trembling*, 28–29.
[11] Grene, M., *op. cit.*, 37–38.

Either/Or Kierkegaard contrasts the aesthetic with the ethical stand-point. In developing the description of the aesthetic life, he writes of the Seducer. The latter keeps an amazing diary recording the total history of a seduction: the most subtle shadings of emotion and interest and the torturous psychologies involved. The ethicist in the second part of *Either/Or* writes edifying letters to the aesthetician. The fantastic irony and humor of Kierkegaard lies in the very composition of such works. They are published under pseudonyms which are not seriously meant to fool anyone; they contain odd inner ironies, such as aestheticist-ethicist, but it is never certain that the letters *are* being written to whom it appears they are intended. One does not know for sure at any point whose side the laugh is on.

It is easily seen that in Kierkegaard we find the first authentic existentialist. His philosophy is directed toward a comprehension of individuality. It faces the human condition but is religiously founded and seeks to locate authentic existence for the Self by facing God and attempting to reach him. The dialectical quality, the irony of Kierkegaard are the strong irrationalism of the thinker. His writing is the testimony to the exhausted categories of Hegelian rationalism; and so it is to be expected that Kierkegaard understands man as a creature who cannot "prove" the existence of God via ontological arguments but leaps to him in an act of ultimate faith.

The strange combination of irrationalism, poetry, irony, and faith constitutes Kierkegaard's passionate paradox. It is a new kind of philosophizing, and yet it is as old as Socrates. We have thus come back to our starting point. It is now possible to determine what Kierkegaard found sympathetic in Socrates. The Socratic dialogue is really astounding: persons talk to persons, they don't rattle categories at each other; there is a simplification of attitude: the dialogue hopes to establish the meaning of Truth, Justice, and the Good. Imagine that these values could derive from a conversation! The astrologer Hegel would have to consult the Absolute!

Swenson once remarked that Kierkegaard never found his poet; but, surely, Kierkegaard found his novelist in Kafka. The piercing works of Kafka are a stubborn testimony to the effort of a writer to deal with the problem of man's guilt. The basic situation Kafka writes about may be seen in his novel, *The Trial.* The story begins:

> "Someone must have been telling lies about Joseph K., for without having done anything wrong he was arrested one fine morning." [12]

K. has been accused. That morning two representatives of the law presented him formally with the accusation. The next step is to learn the details of the charge: of what exactly has he been accused? But to this question the reader finds no answer in the novel.

K. must of necessity find a lawyer to represent him in the courts, yet again the startling fact is that he is making preparations to defend himself against unrevealed charges. And this state of accusation is man's guilt: he must prepare his case before God, take it to the courts, appeal his case to higher authorities, make "deals" with advocates, appeal to hangers-on who pick up bits of information around the courts regarding his case; and he can never penetrate to the highest court, he can never know God, and he is to be condemned and destroyed!

Before his case began, K. was an ordinary citizen, a bank worker, a person who rented quarters, a person who said "hello" to acquaintances, who went about his business. With the accusation K., in being summoned to defend himself in court, is stunned into awareness of himself and the pressing anxiety that accompanies his situation. Quickly he becomes the *defendant*. He realizes soon that his acquaintances are aware of his "case"—aware that he has been accused. Soon K. is isolated. He shuttles to and from his advocate's home. He engages in conversations only with those connected with his case. Another defendant with whom he speaks recalls the large number of people waiting perpetually in the anterooms and outer chambers of the courts.

> " 'I saw all the people in the lobby,' remarked K., 'and thought how pointless it was for them to be hanging about.' 'It's not pointless at all,' said the traveller, 'the only pointless thing is to try taking independent action.' " [13]

There is no "way" for the accused man. He must spend his existence in momentary conversations, blind alleys, fragments of dreams, desperate arguments with advocates and clerks, notes from the lower courts, summonses, and trivial adjudications; there is no withdrawal from one's case—it cannot be dropped. But if independent action is

[12] Kafka, F., *The Trial*, 3.
[13] *Ibid.*, 220–221.

impossible, then K. faces the paradox and the absurdity of being forced to await an unforseeable decision while defending himself on an unknowable charge.

The conclusion of K.'s case is his assassination. There is no other possibility. If a man should stand face to face with an omnipotent diety, is it possible that he should observe anything but his finitude and, therefore, his guilt? The description of K.'s death is the magnificent synthesis of the issues of *The Trial*. At the death-place and moment K.'s

> "glance fell on the top story of the house adjoining the quarry. With a flicker as of a light going up, the casements of a window there suddenly flew open; a human figure, faint and insubstantial at that distance and that height, leaned abruptly far forward and stretched both arms still farther. Who was it? A friend? A good man? Someone who sympathized? Someone who wanted to help? Was it one person only? Or were they all there? Was help at hand? Were there some arguments in his favour that had been overlooked? Of course there must be. Logic is doubtless unshakable, but it cannot withstand a man who wants to go on living. Where was the Judge whom he had never seen? Where was the High Court, to which he had never penetrated? He raised his hands and spread out all his fingers.
>
> "But the hands of one of the partners were already at K.'s throat, while the other thrust the knife into his heart and turned it there twice. With failing eyes K. could still see the two of them, cheek leaning against cheek, immediately before his face, watching the final act. 'Like a dog!' he said; it was as if he meant the shame of it to outlive him." [14]

Kafka's work is one expression of the existentialism of the literary genius; Dostoievski's writings are another. For in them we find equally powerful expression of the issues of salvation and human existence. In the novels of Sartre, however, we have the clearest case of a philosophic existentialist writing existentialist novels. In the literary work of all three writers the chain of thought started by Socrates, emphasized by Pascal, and stated with agonizing force by Kierkegaard, comes to artistic fruition. But at this point we shall turn to the more theoretical formulations of existentialism as they may be found in Sartre's popular lectures and articles.

[14] *Ibid.*, 287–288.

Sartre writes:

> "When we say that man chooses his own self, we mean that every one of us does likewise; but we also mean by that that in making this choice he also chooses all men." [15]

But if in each of our actions we choose an image of man, we are faced with the profound responsibility of accounting for that image; and anguish is the accompaniment of this responsibility.

> "Every man ought to say to himself, 'Am I really the kind of man who has the right to act in such a way that humanity might guide itself by my actions?' And if he does not say that to himself, he is masking his anguish." [16]

If there is no *a priori* essence of man, then all human values are created in the acts of choice. It is no longer meaningful to speak of what we might have done in our lifetime if our dreams had come true. Our potentiality was precisely defined in the acts we performed.

> "For the existentialist there is really no love other than one which manifests itself in a person's being in love. There is no genius other than one which is expressed in works of art; the genius of Proust is the sum of Proust's works; the genuis of Racine is his series of tragedies. Outside of that, there is nothing. Why say that Racine could have written another tragedy, when he didn't write it. A man is involved in life, leaves his impress on it, and outside of that there is nothing." [17]

By the same criterion we cannot speak of a living person as a "coward" or a "failure" or a "hero" in the sense that this person has some inner quality that determines his cowardice or heroism. Cowards and heroes are cowardly or heroic simply in so far as they commit acts of cowardice or heroism. A man who has acted as a beast may definie himself as a human being of dignity if he acts with dignity. We are not condemned to being a failure, but also our past success is continually in the balance, for we must redefine that success as we go along.

[15] Sartre, J–P., *Existentialism*, 20.
[16] *Ibid.*, 24.
[17] *Ibid.*, 38–39.

Existential choice is self-conscious choice. In any case, a choice occurs. If we actively determine it, so much the better; but if we remain passive, then we have chosen passivity—so much the worse! There is no escape from the responsibility of our choice: no one can choose for us.

But one might ask at this point why this philosophy has been termed decadent and morbid.

> "The picture of the world drawn from Existentialist literature is not a rosy one. Some themes recur with a revealing insistence in their novels: nausea (physical and metaphysical), inordinate absorption of hard drinks 'à l'américaine,' homosexuality, abortion, even occasional scatology." [18]

The themes dealt with are the themes of the crisis of our age. Men are bitterly aware of death—an horrific war has been fought. The sudden crises and challenges and betrayals of life during the occupation, the fantastic existence of the underground resistance movement; torture, capture, escape, starvation, the death of love—these were all as immediate as the daily newspaper and the cinema. Moreover, there is on the part of authors like Céline and Henry Miller an awareness which Sartre and the existentialists share—the awareness of a vast ennui, the stifling mud of pretense and bureaucracy that stuffs the streets, the crafty doings of the merchants, the disordered, running social cancer of lives that are groping toward a litle freedom. Within this struggle Sartre, in his novels, addresses the actors and points to a kind of freedom which carries with it the awfulness and trembling of uncertainty when *everything* is at stake. The actors cannot turn to God and they cannot turn to the psychologists; they must choose themselves and construct from the tissue of their own actions the structure of their existence.

It seems that we have reached the logical point for a reconsideration of the tentative definition of existentialism given at the outset of this study. That early definition was derived from Sartre; and it is now clear, I believe, in what sense Sartre intended it. We must now ask: Is this what existentialism is? Have we cut to the heart of the doctrine? Let us proceed cautiously in the investigation at this point.

---

[18] Peyre, H., "Existentialism—A Literature of Despair?", *Yale French Studies*, Spring: Summer (1948), 23.

It is not difficult to observe that there are definite levels of interest and attitude in the literary and philosophic works we have thus far considered. At the literary level we have existentialism discussed or used to explicate the condition of man, to examine his suffering and aloneness and guilt. Writers such as Kafka, Dostoievski, to some extent even Sartre, are shrewd and revealing psychologists as well as literary masters. If we are concerned with descriptions of people, of characters, in specific situations, then few descriptions surpass those of Dostoievski. But such descriptions are literature and not philosophy. They do not concern us here. We turn instead to the philosophical level of existentialism.

Let us leave Kierkegaard in a class by himself. Kierkegaard's problems are those of man's guilt, of his position before God, and of his "fear and trembling" in his finitude. The definition of existentialism as the doctrine of "existence being prior to essence" seems hardly adequate for such a position. To speak of existence and essence in such a stilted style is almost anti-Kierkegaardian in spirit. It smacks of the systematizers, the professors and *Privatdozenten.* If we omit further consideration of Kierkegaard, we are left at the philosophical level with thinkers such as Heidegger, Jaspers, Marcel, and Sartre. Of these men we select Sartre for further study.

It is imperative to recognize several levels of existentialist thought even in Sartre. His novels and popular lectures comprise one level; his technical ontology occupies a different one. The basic confusions and misinterpretations of Sartre's thought are largely due to the confounding of these levels. The novels and lectures are concerned with employing and expositing certain highly technical theories of man's Being: of his human situation and his problems of choice. But the philosophic meaning of such concepts as "situation," "choice," "responsibility," and "anguish" cannot be understood unless they are examined in their proper technical context—as they are developed in Sartre's *L'Être et le Néant.* To comprehend fully the meaning and import of Sartrean existentialism, therefore, we must turn to the background, development, and structure of his ontology, his philosophy of man's Being.

Sartre's philosophy is indebted to the projected ontology of Martin Heidegger. Sartre is Heidegger's best-known follower, and much may be learned about Sartre's existential philosophy by turning briefly to Heidegger's problem.

Heidegger returned in philosophy to the old Aristotelian problem of Being. He is concerned with knowing the nature of Being as Being. The point is clearly stated by Wahl:

> "Heidegger has declared that he is not a philosopher of existence, but a philosopher of Being, and that his eventual aim is ontological. Heidegger considers the problem of existence solely to introduce us to ontology, because the only form of Being with which we are truly in contact (according to Heidegger) is the being of man." [19]

Sartre, too, commences with the problem of Being. His main philosophic work, *Being and Nothingness*, is subtitled "Essay in Phenomenological Ontology." However, the problem of Being for Sartre is not simply a continuation of Heidegger's *Sein und Zeit*, but the attempt to develop an original ontology. For Sartre, the approach to Being turns as much for help to the phenomenology of Husserl and Hegel as to Heidegger. These thinkers have had a profound influence upon Sartre. As Wahl points out, the influence of Husserl in particular leads Sartre "into a kind of idealism which may not be completely consonant with the elements he may have derived from Heidegger." [20] Sartre's interpretation of Being as *en-soi* (in-itself) and as the *pour-soi* (for-itself) betrays the dual tendencies in his thinking; for the *en-soi* corresponds to the realistic element whereas the *pour-soi* corresponds to the idealistic aspect.[21]

For Husserl phenomenology had as its prime purpose the attempt to describe and clarify the content of experience by way of the acts of experiencing. In Heidegger the totality of the acts of the individual determine the individual, and by knowing the former we may know reality. It may be seen, then, that Sartre is in this tradition and is attempting to cut across the traditional positions of idealism and realism in founding a radically new ontology. He is attempting to determine if phenomenology is competent to resolve the problems of ontology.

[19] Wahl, J., *A Short History of Existentialism*, 11; *also see* W. H. Werkmeister, "An Introduction to Heidegger's Existential Philosophy," *Philosophy and Phenomenological Research*, II (1941–2).

[20] Wahl, J., *op. cit.*, 28.

[21] Throughout this work the terms *"pour-soi"* and *"en-soi"* will be used, rather than their English equivalents "for-itself" and "in-itself."

Historically, the Kantian philosophy is the starting point in investigating the phenomenological-existential problem. Varet writes:

> "The failure of the Kantian critique begins with the idea that the theory of the understanding can be developed independently, without an ontology." [22]

For Sartre the question is: Does phenomenology have the inner capacity to expand into an ontology? Sartre's task, therefore, is to determine whether phenomenology can be developed into what Husserl never made of it, namely, a general philosophy. Sartre may then be placed in the Kantian tradition in this sense:

> "In the critical idea, every question about being calls forth the examination of the conditions for knowing it. . . . Thus in Heidegger and in Sartre every philosophic question has the property—it is the very essence of a philosophic question— of going back to the possibles of that question. In this precise sense every conscious existentialist, phenomenologist or not, Sartre in particular, is largely a tributary of the Kantian 'revolution,' which is indeed one of the fundamental acquisitions of modern philosophy. This must be henceforth the distinctive character of every philosophy, to include in its own problem the philosophic enterprise in its totality, and therefore the philosopher himself." [23]

But Sartre faces an even deeper problem in respect to Kant: the issue, namely, of the phenomenon-noumenon dualism. Sartre's two aspects of Being are not parallels to the Kantian dualism, but they nevertheless have been derived only by facing the same issues. Phenomenology goes beyond the Kantian dualism, but it is still possible to ask whether phenomenology is a generalized Kantianism.

If one were now to ask, What is existentialism for Sartre?, the answer would have to be: An ontology which seeks to determine the nature of Being via an investigation of man's Being, thus indebting itself to Heidegger, and which also seeks to determine the complete expression of phenomenology, thus indebting itself to Husserl and Hegel. Ultimately questions of man's choice-situation and his anguish, etc., will come into the picture—but only as derivatives of an

[22] Varet, G., *L'Ontologie de Sartre,* 17.
[23] *Ibid.,* 15.

ontology, involving only peripheral issues. Varet, therefore, is right when he says that "for Sartre the point of departure is not human reality, or existence, or bad faith, or atheism." [24]

Sartre's problem is one of technical philosophy and not of literature or quasi-philosophy. One may talk or write as much as one pleases about Sartre's plays and novels and popular lectures—about human responsibility and the choosing of oneself—and not even come close to the real core of his existentialism. This, of course, is disappointing news for those who considered themselves experts on "existentialism." But did not Sartre himself warn us when he wrote of existentialism:

> "Actually, it is the least scandalous, the most austere of doctrines. It is intended strictly for specialists and philosophers." [25]

In the preceding pages several levels of "existentialism" have been indicated, and only one of these, existentialism as ontology, is the genuine philosophical meaning of the term. A sustained, comprehensive, and critical investigation of Sartre's ontology is the *raison d'être* of this work, which is intended to unquote "existentialism" by considering it as technical ontology.

[24] Varet, *op. cit.*, 2.
[25] Sartre, *op.cit.*, 15.

PART I
Exposition

Chapter I

THE SEARCH FOR BEING

"The concept of 'Being' is the most universal one, as was also realized by Aristotle, Thomas and Hegel; and its universality goes beyond that of any 'genus.' At the same time it is obscure and indefinable; 'Being' cannot be comprehended as anything that is. . . . It cannot be deduced from any higher concepts and it cannot be represented by any lower ones; 'Being' is not something like a being, a stone, a plant, a table, a man. Yet 'Being' seems somehow an evident concept. We make use of it i.. all knowledge, in all our statements, in all our behavior towards anything that 'is,' in our attitude towards ourselves. We are used to living in an 'understanding of Being' . . . but hand in hand with it goes the incomprehensibility of what is meant by 'Being.'"

—Werner Brock

Before beginning our exposition of Sartre's *L'Être et le Néant*, it is necessary to forewarn the reader that both the style and the content of Sartre's main work offer a serious problem in any attempt to present lucidly his ideas and intentions or to translate his language into intelligible English. It is impossible to convey to anyone who has not read *L'Être et le Néant* the involved and often tangled line of Sartre's argument and the horrifying quality of the prose which is intended to convey the author's ideas. In addition to seemingly endless sentences and ambiguous repetitions, the author uses words that do not appear in any dictionary. Sartre invents a new terminology to meet the requirements of the radical ontology he presents. Thus, nouns are used as verbs, and new grammatical constructions are invented to meet the author's needs. What emerges from this strange new language is an ontological structure of Gargantuan length and complexity. We must beg the reader's indulgence in the following pages and hope that he will realize that much of the difficulty of the exposition is necessitated by the nature of the material presented. In many cases it is simply impossible to render the argument in simpler language without danger of doing violence to the meaning Sartre intends to convey to his reader. There has not been a single critic who has written on Sartre's ontology, to our knowledge, who has not commented on the obscurity and complexity of *L'Être et le Néant*.[1] The reader of this work, therefore, who may be only slightly acquainted with Sartre's philosophy, should realize that he is not alone in despairing over these involved arguments and this sometimes fantastic terminology. We hope that our pains in attempting to make this exposition as clear as possible will result in confining the reader's despair to an unavoidable minimum.

To commence our exposition, we may say that "The Search for Being" is a clue to the essential problem with which Sartre is concerned in his attempt to formulate a new ontology. In some sense, the problem of Being has engaged every philosopher and philosophic system under various titles: phenomenon-noumenon, permanence-change, appearance-reality are a few examples. The "Search for Being" may be characterized by a series of questions which Sartre raises throughout *L'Être et le Néant*—such questions as these:

1. What is Being?
2. What is the relation of consciousness to Being?
3. What is the relation of temporality to Being?
4. What is the relation of Nothingness to Being?

The answers to these questions involve, in turn, still further questions which we shall ask as we go along. We are here concerned with a clarification of the questions stated.

---

[1] For example: "It is practically certain that one could count on the fingers of one hand those who have had the patience to read every line of *L'Être et le Néant*, and fewer still is the number of those who can in all honesty claim that they have always understood it,"—Foulquié, P., *Existentialism*, 41. Also, *L'Être et le Néant* is described as "exceedingly long, over 700 large and closely printed pages, always difficult and often obscure."—Ayer, A. J., "Novelist–Philosophers: V—Jean–Paul Sartre," *Horizon*, Vol. XII, No. 67 (1945), 12.

1. WHAT IS BEING?

In the attempt to penetrate to the "heart" of Being, Sartre first considers the answers modern thought has given to the problem of Being. He examines and discards a series of historical dualisms. Sartre throws out as inadequate the dualisms of interior-exterior, appearance-being, potency-act, appearance-essence, and, finally, phenomenon-noumenon.

For Sartre, a preliminary definition of Being is, in a sense, impossible; at least, its possibility would involve us either in paradoxes or in an infinite regress. If we mean by 'definition,' in part, a listing of predicates which describe the object, then such a listing cannot be attempted so far as Being is concerned; for, as we shall show later, the ascription of any predicate involves us in the problem of the being of *the predicate ascribed.* We should thus have to define the being of the being of the predicate, and the being of the being of that being, *ad infinitum.* For Sartre, the phenomenological method provides an approach to the nature of Being.

Taken in its most fundamental sense, phenomenology is a direct "looking upon" or inspection of the givens of sensory experience. Such inspection confronts us, first of all, with "appearances." These appearances *are*—in the sense, namely, that we are presented with them. They would not be appearances unless they appeared. But if these appearances *are*, then, according to Sartre, we have located Being; for appearance *is* Being. Thus, if appearance *is*, "Being *is*." The object in appearance *is;* and "that is the sole manner of defining its way of Being." [2]

2. WHAT IS THE RELATION OF CONSCIOUSNESS TO BEING?

It is essential to the understanding of Sartre's doctrine of Being that we distinguish between two realms of Being, the *en-soi* and the *pour-soi.* In the introduction we said that the *pour-soi* corresponds to the idealistic element in Being, and the *en-soi* to the realistic element. This statement requires clarification.

The *pour-soi*, in its most simple sense, is consciousness. For Sartre, speculation begins in subjectivity; more specifically, it begins with the Cartesian *cogito*, which is taken to be the root of all judgments and all cognition. It is "an absolute truth founded upon the immediate

---

[2] Sartre, *L'Être et le Néant*, 15. (Hereafter the abbreviation "EN" will be used).

grasp which consciousness has of itself, and as such is the basis for all other certain truths."[3] Sartre recognizes, however, that there is a pre-reflective as well as a reflective *cogito,* and that through the examination of the pre-reflective *cogito,* we may come to a general understanding of the other pole of Being, the *en-soi.*

Moreover, the pre-reflective *cogito* is the basis for the reality of consciousness; for there can be no consciousness where there is no reference to an object.[4] Consciousness cannot exist apart from its active unfolding in the acts of consciousness.[5] Consciousness is thus the cause of its own manner of Being and is the identity of appearance and existence. Consciousness exists to the extent to which it "appears"; and the absoluteness of consciousness consists in the identity of its appearance and existence. Sartre's recourse to the pre-reflective *cogito,* therefore, enables him to escape from the infinite regress of "knowing-known"; for the "coincidence of existence and appearance indicates that the pre-reflective *cogito* is an absolute in the order of existence and a condition of all knowledge." [6]

Consciousness is more than self-reflection; all consciousness is consciousness *of* something. Consciousness intends some object in the world. What is intended, Sartre asserts, is some "trans-phenomenal" Being beyond consciousness. The realm of transphenomenal Being is the realm of the *en-soi.* For Sartre, the *en-soi* is the rough is-ness of Being, the brute confrontation of Being, the "stuff" of the world. Thus, the Being of consciousness faces the Being of the phenomenon: the *pour-soi* faces the *en-soi,* and although both may be identified by an analysis of subjectivity, they remain alien and severed realms. If we tentatively defined the *pour-soi* as consciousness, we may tentatively define the *en-soi* as the transphenomenal Being of the object. Whether contact between these realms is possible is one of the profound problems Sartre faces in his analysis.

By constructing an "ontological argument in reverse," Sartre tries to demonstrate the existence of the transphenomenal Being of the object from the pre-reflective *cogito;* for consciousness, he argues, implies in its very Being a non-conscious, transphenomenal Being. Conscious-

[3] Collins, J., "The Existentialism of J-P. Sartre," *Thought,* Vol. XXIII, No. 88, (March, 1948), 69.

[4] EN, 19.

[5] *Ibid.,* 19-21.

[6] Collins, *op. cit.,* 69.

ness, Sartre holds, is a Being which, because it is in question in its own Being, implies a Being other than itself.[7] The definition of consciousness which Sartre ultimately establishes is the following: the *pour-soi* (consciousness) is that which it is not, and is not that which it is. We intend to explicate fully the nature and meaning of this paradoxical conception of consciousness.

3. WHAT IS THE RELATION OF TEMPORALITY TO BEING?

The consciousness with which we are concerned, the *pour-soi*, is not static; it is "passionately involved in temporality." In fact, the *pour-soi* exists only because it has a future. Sartre's discussion of temporality reveals the deeper relation between consciousness and Being. He says that the Being of the *pour-soi* will be elucidated only when we have defined and described the signification of the temporal. "It is only then that we shall be able to arrive at the study of the problem which occupies us: that of the original relation of consciousness with Being." [8]

What, then, is the relation of temporality to Being? For Sartre, temporality is an original synthesis containing structured moments.[9] To understand temporality it is necessary to pursue a phenomenological analysis of the dimensions of temporality: past, present, and future.

Let us consider a few sentences: I am the person you now see; I am the person you saw last Monday; I was the man who owned that white bulldog. The difficulty is: in what sense is it possible to speak of one's present self as the self that *was* at place P at time T? Is it the same self? Was it the same self? This tie between the present self and the past self must be explained. In what sense do I remain the same self, able to be both "was" and "is"?

Sartre holds that temporality cannot be artificially split up into past and present. There must be an ontological connection between them. "The term 'was' designates . . . the ontological leap from the present into the past and represents an original synthesis of these two modes of temporality." [10] "Was" is the ontological liaison of the *pour-*

---

[7] EN, 29.
[8] *Ibid.*, 149.
[9] *Ibid.*, 150.
[10] *Ibid.*, 158.

soi; what Sartre terms the "facticity" of the *pour-soi* is it pastness.[11]
The facticity of the *pour-soi* is threatened and encroached upon by the
en-soi; the latter attempts to "swallow" it up. The "was" characterizes
the type of Being of the *pour-soi:* "The relation of the *pour-soi* to its
Being. The past is the *en-soi* which I am, considered as passed beyond." [12]

In the present-past relationship a dialectic is involved: "I was the
man who owned that white bulldog." This means that I am the man
who "was the man." But in the same sense in which I am the man who
was, I certainly am not the man who was; for I am the man I am. The
internal connection in this dialectic of "am," "was," and "am not" is
the relation "not to be." It follows, then, that if "I *am* not my own past,
it cannot be in the original mode of becoming, but in so far as *I have
to be it in order not to be it* and *I have not to be it in order to be it.*" [13]
Sartre concludes that, in regard to my Being, "I am in the mode of
internal liaison with the *not to be.*" [14]

The dialectic of present-past reveals the relation between the two
realms of Being: the *pour-soi,* when it becomes pastness, is seized by
the *en-soi* and rendered pastness or "facticity," as Sartre puts it. But
since the present *is pour-soi,* a paradox is involved: although we must
define the present in terms of Being, whenever we attempt to specify
the present, we are left with only an infinitesimal instant, a Nothingness. Here is the fundamental contradiction of existence: we always
find the indissoluble pair, Being and Nothingness.

The problem of the present forces us to expand our understanding
of the *pour-soi.* The *pour-soi,* as present, cannot be seized as such;
it is in a state of flight. Sartre says that the present is a perpetual flight
in the face of Being and that whenever we experience the present it is
under the form of flight. We cannot truly seize the present in any of
its instants, for these instants themselves are in flight.[15]

The present, however, is as yet imperfectly understood, for we have
considered only one half of its dialectical relation. In addition to
flight *from,* there must be flight *to.* The *pour-soi* has a facticity, but

[11] EN, 162.
[12] *Ibid.*
[13] *Ibid.,* 161.
[14] *Ibid.*
[15] *Ibid.,* 168.

it also has a future.[16] Sartre's theory of the nature of futurity is complex. The Sartrean future is the *pour-soi's* unavoidable though in-
determinate Being-to-be. This future is not some chronologically
ordered or homogeneous succession of instants to come.[17] Futurity is
the paradoxical mixture of what I shall be and yet what that shall-be
is not. Just as the dialectic of past-present entails an ontological liaison
of "was-ness," so the dialectic of present-future depends upon the
ontological connective of "flight." Flight from present Being toward
future Being outlines the skeleton of the shall-be, although it does not
cause or mold that shall-be.

Since "the future is that which I have to be in so far as I am able
not to be it," [18] and since "the future is myself in so far as I await myself as presence at a being beyond being," [19] Sartre asserts that the
pour-soi of the present reveals the *pour-soi* yet to be. The latter is
held before the *pour-soi* as its image-to-be. In this sense the not-yet has
Being, and its Being is that of futurity. The future world "has meaning as future only in so far as I am present in it as *an other* which I
shall be, in another physical, affective, social, and so on, position." [20]
Sartre concludes that "I must . . . 'become what I was', but it is in a
world itself *become* that I must become it, and in a world become
from what it is." [21]

From the total unity of past, present, and future, with the ontological liaisons of "was-ness" and "flight" which bind them together
dialectically, arises the Self. The Self holds within it the problem of
its freedom, for the flight of the *pour-soi* toward its future is its measure
of freedom to become what it will be. But this freedom is unique: the
pour-soi does not accept or reject its freedom in a purely conceptual
fashion. The *pour-soi* faces its own "problematicity." [22] "The future
constitutes the meaning of my present *pour-soi,* as the project of its
possibility, but it does not predetermine in any way my *pour-soi* to
come, since the *pour-soi* is always abandoned in this 'nihilating'
(*néantisante*) obligation to be the foundation of its nothingness." [23]

[16] EN, 168.
[17] *Ibid.,* 174.
[18] *Ibid.,* 170.
[19] *Ibid.,* 172.
[20] *Ibid.,* 171.
[21] *Ibid.,* 172.
[22] *Ibid.,* 174.
[23] *Ibid.,* 173.

Sartre concludes that the *pour-soi* cannot avoid its "problematic-ity," since the *pour-soi* itself is problematic in the sense of continually being faced by an uncertain future. This is what Sartre means when he asserts that Man is a Being whose meaning is always problematic. Thus, "the *pour-soi* can never be anything but problematically its future, for it is separated from that future by a nothingness which it itself is: in a word, the *pour-soi* is free and its freedom is to itself its own limit." [24] To be free, Sartre says, is to be condemned to be free.[25]

4. WHAT IS THE RELATION OF NOTHINGNESS TO BEING?

We have thus far attempted to answer the question, "What is Being?" If we now ask, "What is non-Being?", we have hinted at the nature of Nothingness; for to each question we ask there exists the possibility of a negative answer.[26] Sartre considers several varieties of non-Being.

The non-Being of knowing is of a conceptual order. If I say "the dog is not the cat," I am, according to Sartre, formulating a purely conceptual negation. However, if I say "Pierre is not here" after I have expected to find him here and have looked for him here, then I am uttering a negation which is not purely conceptual. The difference between these two types of non-Being is that the "non-Being" of Pierre has a Being, it *is* a Nothingness.

Sartre explains the Being of Nothingness in the following example: Let us say that Pierre has not waited for me at an appointment. I came to the place where we were supposed to have met, and "I immediately saw that he was not there." Was there, then, an intuition of Pierre's absence? When I looked at the scene where I was supposed to meet Pierre, everything I saw underwent a "nihilation" (*néantisation*).

I am at this moment looking for Pierre; as I look about me at the scene where he is supposed to be, there is, for me, a successive disappearance of objects, Sartre says,—of those objects which are *not* Pierre. The "nihilated" form of Pierre rises between my look and the objects upon which my look is directed. The Nothingness of Pierre is in opposition to the Nothingness of the crumbled objects, because the Nothingness of Pierre "haunts" the scene.[27]

---

[24] EN, 173–174.
[25] Cf. *ibid.*
[26] *Ibid.*, 39.
[27] *Ibid.*, 45.

This non-conceptual Nothingness has a certain structure which the purely conceptual Nothingness does not have. If, after I have determined that Pierre is absent, I say to myself, "Well, George Washington isn't here either," there arises no constitution of the Nothingness of George Washington. Such a negation is simply a thought and does not produce non-Being.[28]

Being has priority over Nothingness in the sense that there can be Being without Nothingness, but there can be no Nothingness unless there has been Being. Whereas Hegel says that Being and Nothingness are equally empty abstractions, Sartre holds that although Being is empty of every determination other than identity with itself, non-Being is empty *of Being*. "In a word, what is necessary here to recall against Hegel is that being *is* and that nothingness *is not*." [29]

We may now ask, "Where does Nothingness come from?" Sartre also raises the associated question, "What must man be in his being in order that through him Nothingness comes to Being?" Sartre reveals the "secret" of Nothingness. He says that "it is necessary to find the foundation of all negation in a 'nihilation' which would be exercised *at the very core of immanence;* it is in absolute immanence, in the pure subjectivity of the instantaneous *cogito,* that we must discover the original act by which man is to himself his own nothingness." [30]

In what sense is the instantaneous or pre-reflective *cogito* the basis of all negation? We said earlier that the pre-reflective *cogito* is the basis for the reality of consciousness and that the reality of consciousness depends on its being presented with a known object. Original negation or Nothingness arises from the pre-reflective *cogito* because *the cogito* is *not* before it meets its known object. To put it in another way: when Sartre says[31] that, in rising from the heart of Being, consciousness creates and sustains its essence—the synthetic arrangement of its possibilities—he implies that the pre-reflective consciousness *is* only in so far as it does realize its possibilities. But if the possibilities are "possibles," (i.e., if they lie in the future), then the possibility of their not being realized exists; this is negation in its root form.

[28] EN, 46–47.
[29] *Ibid.,* 51.
[30] *Ibid.,* 83.
[31] *Ibid.,* 21.

Sartre distinguishes between two types of nihilation. There is the nihilating structure of the pre-reflective *cogito*. Consciousness "*is not* its own motive in so far as it is *empty* of all content." [32] This emptiness of content is what has been described above as the root-negation of as yet unrealized "possibles."

Although the original negation which arises from the pre-reflective *cogito* is the basis of all negation, there is a second type of nihilation which is the nihilating structure of temporality. Of this second type Sartre says that "the consciousness is confronted with its past and its future as confronted with a self which it is in the mode of not-being."[33] This is the area of negation which circumscribes the core of the *pour-soi*. It is the Nothingness of that which separates the *pour-soi* from its past and from its future. The Nothingness of the *pour-soi* is, for Sartre, the possibility of freedom. Freedom is the "possibility for the human reality to secrete a nothingness which isolates it" [34] and "freedom is the human being putting its past outside of the game in secreting its own nothingness." [35]

Nothingness reveals freedom and also reveals our anguish. "It is in anguish that man becomes conscious of his freedom or, if one prefers, anguish is the mode of being of freedom as consciousness of being; it is in anguish that freedom is in its being in question for itself." [36]

Anguish must be distinguished from fear. The latter is of things of the world, but anguish is anguish before oneself, fear of having fear, consciousness of freedom. Sartre gives the example of a person walking along a narrow, dangerous path, who considers the various possibilities of catastrophe: the earth giving way, a landslide, slipping on a rock, and so on. These imagined catastrophies are general; they might happen to anyone walking along such a path. But as soon as our protagonist on the path considers these possibilities as *his* possibilities —that *he* might slip and fall to his death—then he experiences fear. The distinction between fear and anguish is that fear has a specific object, but anguish is anguish before one's "possibles"—no specific one having been selected. Fear of having fear is anguish because it is fear

[32] EN, 72.
[33] *Ibid.*
[34] *Ibid.,* 61.
[35] *Ibid.,* 65.
[36] *Ibid.,* 66.

of the non-specific. Anxiety has no ascertained object, and that is the piercing hurt of the anguish.

When Sartre says that anguish is the self-awareness of "possibles" as *my* "possibles," he does not mean that the awareness of these "possibles" is a conceptual act which occurs prior to some involvement with those situations of which the "possibles" are a part. Rather, we act in situations which reveal "possibles" in the process of being realized. We are referred back to the meaning of the "possibles," but we do not experience the awareness of "possibles" in a purely beforehand, or abstract sense. Man is a creature *involved* in his reality. He does not gaze upon it as a Martian might coolly consider earthman's works—he is inextricably a part of reality. We are engaged in our reality, hurled into the world and involved in it. "This means that we act before positing our 'possibles' " [37] We discover ourselves, then, in a world peopled with exigencies, and we are at the core of projects in the course of realization. Thus, man turns up in the world—he appears on the scene.[38]

Sartre, in concerning himself with the profound problem of Being *qua* Being, has found it necessary to investigate man's being in order to penetrate to the heart of Being. He has considered temporality, consciousness, and Nothingness as dimensions of the dialectic of Being. The problem has been to resolve the basic dualism of the two realms of Being, the *pour-soi* and the *en-soi*.

It may be seen that the *pour-soi* is in flight both toward the future and from the past, and, further, that it is separated from both by the Nothingness which establishes its freedom and, at the same time, its anguish. The *pour-soi*, as consciousness, is man's possibility of freedom, for in self-reflection and self-awareness lie the roads of freedom. But the *en-soi* is quite the opposite of the *pour-soi;* it is unreflective, stolid, and gross—brute packed-togetherness.[39]

In Sartre's novel *Nausea*, the protagonist, Roquentin, suddenly grasps the reality of existence in its brute *en-soi* as he is seated on a park

---

[37] EN, 75.

[38] *Existentialism, op. cit.*, 18.

[39] Collins, *op. cit.*, 77–78. Sartre "describes the *en-soi* as a massive, crammed-down bulk of being which quite brutally *is*. It allows for no self-acquaintance with its own reality because of its opacity and thickness. Only in a loose sense can the In-self be called a self, for it supports no relations with others and allows for no presence to itself and self-development of its own solid plenitude."

bench one day. In an almost perverse Husserlian fashion the normal world is bracketed off, and he perceives the park and its objects as a swollen blob of jelly-like consistency, which presses in on him like quicksand about a sinking man.[40] The experience of the *en-soi* in its unexpurgated immediacy is "nausea." The flight of the *pour-soi*, then, is the flight from this nauseous *en-soi* toward futurity. But futurity itself has *en-soi* as part of its Being. Thus, man is in flight from *en-soi* toward *en-soi;* this is the tragedy of his condition. Man in his flight is haunted by Being, yet he cannot absorb that Being under pain of the engulfment of his *pour-soi*. "The human reality in its being is suffering because it arises to being as perpetually haunted by a totality which it is without power to be, since precisely it could not reach the *en-soi* without losing itself as *pour-soi*." [41]

The *pour-soi* is in a vicious paradox: since it is *lack*, it is hurled toward the future; yet if it fills itself with *en-soi*, it nauseates itself. In like fashion, we can retreat into the past only at the risk of absorbing the *en-soi* of facticity: we slip away into the *en-soi* and so yield our freedom, our authenticity. The dilemma of the *pour-soi* is the urgent condition of human existence. If freedom of the *pour-soi* is freedom only within the confines of this condition, and if man is condemned to this strange and awful freedom, then Sartre's great burden in the remainder of his research on Being and Nothingness must be the explanation of how man operates in his Being and how he may both choose and realize his "possibles."

---

[40] Sartre, J-P., "The Root of the Chestnut Tree," *Partisan Review*, (Winter, 1946), 32–33. "Was it a dream, that enormous presence? It was there, poised over the park, tumbling from the trees, all soft, gluing up everything, a thick gelatinous mass. And was I in it, I, and the entire park? I was afraid, but above all I was furious, it seemed so stupid, so inappropriate. I despised that ignoble jelly. It was everywhere! It reached to the sky, it spread out in all directions, it filled everything with its sprawling mass, and I could see layer upon layer of it, extending much farther than the limits of the park and the houses and Bouville. I was no longer in Bouville, nor anywhere, I was floating. I was not surprised; I was very well aware that it was the World, the naked World which had suddenly shown itself, and I was choking with rage against this huge absurd being. . . . I cried out: 'What a filthy mess, what a mess!' and I shook myself to throw off the sticky slime but it clung to me and there was so much of it, tons and tons of existence, endless tons: I was suffocating under the weight of a tremendous ennui."

[41] EN, 134.

Chapter II

THE OTHER

In the first part of *L'Être et le Néant* Sartre described mainly the Being of the *pour-soi* and its relation to the *en-soi*. This study, however, has left him with the necessity of rescuing his ontology from the charge of solipsism, for he has explicated only the Being of one's consciousness with no bridge established to the consciousness of Others. The danger is that "Sartre has followed so closely the idealistic conception of Self-consciousness (*cogito*) as the transcendental origin and 'creator' of all Being that he constantly faces the danger of transcendental solipsism." [1] In facing the problem of solipsism in EN, Sartre analyzes the existence of the Other and the relations between my Being and the Being of the Other. [2]

1. THREE THEORIES OF THE OTHER

In his analysis of the "Reef of Solipsism" Sartre takes into consideration the theories of the Other held by Husserl, Hegel, and Heidegger before presenting his own views.

a) Husserl.—"Husserl's main argument—as Sartre sees it—consists in the thesis that the reference to the Other is a necessary condition for the existence of the world." [3] Husserl, according to Sartre, has defined the Other as an "absence." How, Sartre asks, is it possible to have an intuition of an absence? Unless I arbitrarily presuppose that the Other is identical with me, true knowledge of the Other escapes me. [4]

---

[1] Marcuse, H., "Existentialism: Remarks on Jean–Paul Sartre's *L'Être et le Néant*," *Philosophy and Phenomenological Research*, Vol. VIII (1947–1948), 316.

[2] EN, 277.

[3] Schuetz, A., "Sartre's Theory of the Alter Ego," *Philosophy and Phenomenological Research*, Vol. IX, No. 2, (1948), 183.

[4] *Ibid.*, 184.

The inadequacy of the Husserlian theory of the Other is that phenomenological method operates only through reducing the object via the self's analysis and through intending the object via the self's acts of intending. But since we cannot penetrate beyond the core of the self, the Other escapes us. "The only liaison which Husserl has been able to establish between my being and that of the other is that of the *understanding*; he could not then . . . escape from solipsism." [5]

b) Hegel.—For Hegel the problem of the Other is the problem of consciousness of self. Sartre quotes Hegel: "The consciousness of self is real only in so far as it knows its echo (and its reflection) in another." [6] For Hegel, Sartre claims, the existence of my consciousness as consciousness of self depends on the appearance of the Other. Self-consciousness appears with the *excluding* of the Other. [7] "Such exclusion takes a double form: By the very fact of being myself, I exclude the Other; by the very fact of being himself, the Other, whom I exclude, excludes me." [8]

Sartre accuses Hegel on two counts: first, of "epistemological optimism" and, second, of "ontological optimism." According to Sartre, it appears to Hegel "that the *truth* of the consciousness of self can appear, that is, that an objective accord can be realized between the consciousness under the name of recognition of me by the Other and of the Other by me." [9] The "ontological optimism" is an even more fundamental element in Hegelian philosophy. The essence of this optimism, according to Sartre, is the Hegelian assertion that the truth of the All already exists, permitting, therefore, the claim that the truth regarding the Other is possible to obtain. [10]

---

[5] EN, 291.
[6] *Ibid.*, 293.
[7] *Ibid.*, 291.
[8] Schuetz, *op. cit.*, 185.
[9] EN, 296.
[10] *Ibid.*, 299. "Truth is truth of the All. And he places himself at the point of the truth, that is, of the All, in order to envisage the problem of the other. Thus, when the Hegelian monism considers the relation of the consciousnesses, it is not to be placed in any particular consciousness. Although the All is to be realized, it is already there as the truth of all that is true; also, when Hegel writes that every consciousness being identical with itself is other than the other, he has established himself in the All, outside of consciousness and considers consciousnesses from the point of view of the Absolute."

The failure of Hegel's optimism is the failure to produce the basis of intersubjective knowledge (knowledge of the Other). Hegel is left with a mere plurality of consciousnesses which cannot be properly connected. Hegel's optimism is the illusion that such a connection has been established in his arguments concerning the Other.[11]

c) Heidegger.—It is also necessary to point out that the question of the Other arises for a person, according to Sartre's exposition of Heidegger's thought, only when that person has achieved authentic existence. Authenticity is achieved in the resolute decision the individual makes regarding his possibility of death. At the moment that the individual chooses his authenticity, he is disclosed to himself in authenticity, and the Others around him are at the same moment elevated toward the authentic.[12]

Sartre charges that Heidegger's description of the Other is an ontic and psychologistic description and not a true ontological explanation, since he claims there is no warranty for passing from the idea of being-with to the ontological structure of being-in-the-world.[13] Sartre holds that Heidegger, like Husserl and Hegel, has failed to produce an acceptable theory of the Other and that Heidegger's philosophy leaves the problem unsolved: it leaves the self isolated in the dungeon of solipsism—in "solitary."

In general, Sartre is dissatisfied with the positions of both realism and idealism in so far as they have taken stands on the problem of intersubjectivity. Through a dialectical examination of the problem in both idealist and realist camps,[14] he concludes that both positions lead to paradox and internal contradiction; for the realist position, when followed through, leads necessarily to idealism, whereas idealism, when it abandons the solipsist hypothesis, leads to a dogmatic and

---

[11] EN, 299, "The optimism of Hegel results in a defeat: between the object-other and me-subject, there is no common measure, no more than between the consciousness (of) self and the consciousness *of* the other. I cannot know myself *in* the other if the other is first object for me and I can no more seize the other in its true being, that is, in its subjectivity. No universal consciousness can be derived from the relation of the consciousnesses. It is what we shall call their ontological separation."

[12] *Ibid.*, 303.

[13] *Ibid.*, 304.

[14] *Ibid.*, 277–288.

totally unjustified realism.[15] The problem of the Other, according to Sartre, can, therefore, be solved by neither idealism nor realism.

2. THE LOOK

Any attempt to explore intersubjectivity, Sartre asserts, must commence with the *cogito*. We cannot prove the existence of the Other in the sense of logical proof. The Other is immediately known, or, as Sartre puts it, "encountered." "The existence of the Other has the nature of a contingent and irreducible fact." [16] We, therefore, cannot ontologically derive the existence of the Other.[17] Such is the general outline of Sartre's theory of the Other's existence.[18]

If the *cogito* is to be the starting point, then Sartre commits himself to the position that any consideration of the Other must begin wih the Being of the self.[19] Also, he holds that the rapport with the Other will be a relationship of Being to Being and not one of understanding to understanding.[20] Husserl failed by measuring Being by the understanding, Hegel failed in identifying understanding with Being.[21] Sartre, to the contrary, proposes to give an explanation of the relationship between my Being and the Being of the Other.[22]

In the affirmation of the existence and presence of the Other, taken now as a relation of Being to Being, the question which initiates the Sartrean inquiry into the specific problem of the Other arises: "Is there in the everyday reality an original relation to the Other which

[15] EN, 285.
[16] *Ibid.*, 307.
[17] Marcuse, *op. cit.*, 316.
[18] Schuetz, *op. cit.*, 187. "Sartre formulates the following criteria for a valid theory of the Other's existence. 1. Such a theory need not *prove* the Other's existence, the affirmation of which is rooted in a 'pre-ontological' understanding. 2. The Cartesian *cogito* is the only possible point of departure in order to find (not reasons for my belief in the Other's existence, but) the Other himself as being-not-me. 3. The Other does not have to be grasped as an object of our cogitations, but in his existence 'for us' as affecting our actual concrete being. 4. The Other has to be conceived as being 'not me,' but this negation is not an external spatial one; it is an internal negation, defined by Sartre as a synthetic and active connection between two terms, either of which constitutes itself by negating the other."
[19] EN, 300.
[20] *Ibid.*, 300–301.
[21] *Ibid.*
[22] *Ibid.*, 311.

can be constantly sought and which, consequently, can be disclosed to me, outside of all reference to a religious or mystical unknowable?" [23]

The basis of the original relation to the Other is the very *appearance* of the Other in my world: he appears to me. A shock accompanies the presentation of the Other to my world. "The appearance among the objects of *my* universe of an element of disintegration of this universe is what I call the appearance of *a* man in my universe."[24] The Other shocks my world in an original, unique, and irreducible manner: he *looks at me*.[25] "At each instant the Other *looks at me*." [26] The basis of the solution to the problem of the Other will be the *Look*. But "what does it mean for me: *to be seen?*" [27]

Sartre asserts that shame reveals to the self the Look of the Other.[28] The Other looks at me and, in the Look, shocks or "haemorrhages" my inner unity, my inner world, my subjectivity. The recovery of this inner world of the self is possible by a retaliation against the Other; i.e., by making the Other the object of *my* Look and destroying his inner unity. By the Look of the Other I have been made an object for his subjectivity, and he knows me only as object, never as subject. In the same manner, I know the Other as object, never as subject.[29]

Consciousness of being object exists when the Other looks at me, but does it also exist when the Other is absent? Absence is defined by Sartre as a mode of Being of the human-reality that was originally determined by presence.[30] That is, I look for somebody because he is generally there. But what is important in consciousness of being object, or of being the one who looks for the Other in his absence, is that in these cases we are being-for-other. Thus, "the look has placed us on the track of our being-for-other and it has revealed to us the indubitable existence of this otherself for which we are." [31]

I "cannot be object for an object";[32] I must be object for a subject. But if my being-for-other has revealed the necessity for the Other, the

[23] EN, 311.
[24] *Ibid.*, 312.
[25] *Ibid.*, 315.
[26] *Ibid.*
[27] *Ibid.*, 316.
[28] *Ibid.*, 319.
[29] *Ibid.*, 327–328.
[30] *Ibid.*, 337.
[31] *Ibid.*, 342.
[32] *Ibid.*, 349.

question remains: What is the Being of the being-for-other?[33] Sartre asserts that the being-for-other is not an ontological structure of the *pour-soi*.[34] "We cannot even think of deriving, as a consequence of a principle, the being-for-other from the being-for-self, nor, reciprocally, the being-for-self from the being-for-other." [35] Sartre's answer to our question will be given later, when the ground for such an answer has been prepared.

We may return now to the concept of shame and its relation to the problem of the Other. Pure shame, Sartre tells us, is the feeling of being *an* object, not some particular object. Shame exists when I recognize myself as degraded by and dependent upon the Other. "Shame is the feeling of *original fall*, not from the fact that I would have committed such and such a fault, but simply from the fact that I am 'fallen' into the world, in the midst of things, and that I need the mediation of the other in order to be what I am." [36]

Partly, then, through the experience of shame, I seek the overthrow of the Other by appropriating him as object for my subjectivity. But in this appropriation I hope to achieve more than simply the objectification of the Other. What I seek is no less than the discovery in the Other of an aspect of myself: my objectivity.

But the explication of the being-for-Other has been carried as far as possible within the limits of the structures of Being examined. A dilemma has resulted: the Other "seizes" me in my facticity as object, and I can never "seize" the Other in his subjectivity. If I attempt to prove the latter, my proof founders on the reefs of the limits of my knowledge; and if I accept the facticity of the Other as object, I fail to penetrate to his core.

3. THE BODY

Sartre's argument regarding the Other can be carried no further in its present framework; it is necessary to investigate a series of new levels of the structure of Being.

If we return to the very first knowledge of the Other, it will be recalled that the Other appears to us. The appearance of the Other is possible only in so far as he originally appears manifested as a *body*.

[33] EN, 342.
[34] *Ibid.*
[35] *Ibid.*
[36] *Ibid.*, 349.

If "this object that the Other is for me and this object that I am for the Other are manifested *as bodies*,"[37] then Sartre asks, What is my body? and What is the body of the Other? [38]

My body has a dualistic aspect: it is "either a thing among things, or else it is that by which the things are disclosed to me." [39] My body cannot be both of these two aspects at the same time.[40] Because of this double relation, I may be present to a part of my body without its *being me* or my *being it*. This double relation derives from the fact that I cannot sense one of my organs sensing. I cannot see my eye seeing. When I do "seize" my eye, it is as an aspect of the world—an object for me—or else "it is that by which . . . things are disclosed to me." [41] There are, then, two aspects of the investigation of the body that can be delineated: the body as being-for-self and the body as being-for-Other.

Sartre asserts that the understanding itself is a self-contradictory element if it is unrelated to positional experience. The understanding must be involved; i.e., it must be understanding of something somewhere.[42]

"To be for the human reality is *to-be-there*; that is, 'there, on that chair,' 'there, at that table,' 'there, at the top of that mountain, with those dimensions, that orientation, etc.' " [43] The necessity of the positional element in experience (being-*there*) involves, however, an ambiguity: "On the one hand . . . if it is necessary that I may be under the form of being-there, it is completely contingent that I am, for I am not the foundation of my being; on the other hand, if it is necessary that I may be engaged in such and such a point of view, it is contingent that it is precisely this one, to the exclusion of every other." [44] Sartre terms this double contingency the "facticity" of the *pour-soi*. We used the term "facticity" earlier in the exposition of Sartre's definition of the *pour-soi* as not being what it is and being what it is not. The *pour-soi* can never know itself in itself, for at the foundation of itself is its Nothingness.[45]

---

[37] EN, 364.
[38] *Ibid.*
[39] *Ibid.*, 366.
[40] *Ibid.*
[41] *Ibid.*
[42] *Ibid.*
[43] *Ibid.*, 371.
[44] *Ibid.*
[45] *Ibid.*

The individuation of the *pour-soi* is realized through its body. "The body is a necessary characteristic of the *pour-soi*; it . . . proceeds necessarily from the nature of the *pour-soi* that it is body." [46] The body appears to Others. The world in which it appears is given to the *pour-soi* as positional to it, not simply as an experential "possible," or a cognitive expectation. In so far as I am given to the world, I am given through my body. "To say that I am entered into the world, 'come to the world,' or that there is a world or that I have a body, is one sole and selfsame thing." [47]

The world, for Sartre, is given to me through its *utensil* quality and its resistance to my actions toward it. This means that the desk in front of me is desk-to-be-written-upon, not simply "desk," and the Others, in the same fashion, are Others-for-me. The objectivity of the world resides in the synthetic unity of the utensils which comprise it and not in creative power of a subjectivity. "Thus, the world appears to me as objectively articulated: it never refers back to a creative subjectivity but to the infinity of utensil complexes." [48]

An example which Sartre gives clarifies the utensil-quality of the world.[49] The statement "Carthage is to be destroyed" has the indifferentness of an unoriented, referenceless proposition. The meaning of the destruction of Carthage is one thing for the Romans, but quite another for the Carthagenians. For the Romans, Carthage is to be destroyed, but for the Carthagenians, Carthage is to be enslaved. Thus, meanings are always meanings *in situo*, related to persons . . . involved. In their totality these utensils reveal more than objectivity: they are objects which *resist us*. "What I perceive when I wish to draw this glass to my mouth is not my effort, it is its *heaviness*, that is, its resistance toward entering into a utensil complex, which I have made appear in the world." [50]

The resistance of utensils to the *pour-soi* reveals the nature of the position of the *pour-soi* in the world. There is a dialectic of interaction between the objects, the Others, and the Self. This dialectic can-

---

[46] EN, 372.
[47] *Ibid.*, 381.
[48] *Ibid.*, 387.
[49] *Ibid.*
[50] *Ibid.*, 389.

not posit a body apart from the objects which are utensils for and resistants to that body.[51]

The body involves infinitely more than simply the flesh I inhabit. My body in its being-for-Others is the synthetic resultant of my "seizing" of the totality of utensils given to me and, in addition, my seizing of Others as they condition my experience with *their* attitudes, interests, and passions. The way in which objects are disclosed to me will then depend on my birth, my race, my class, my nationality, my physiological structure, etc., in so far as these elements themselves are constituted by my relationships to Others. This also is a dialectical relation, for I am not simply conditioned into class, nationality, etc., but pass beyond such conditioning and, in the passing beyond, establish the synthetic unity of my being-in-the-world.

Sartre is now able to relate the conception of body to choice and both to freedom.

Sartre holds that we choose the manner in which we "exist" [52] ourselves. The *pour-soi* "exists" its body and thereby chooses its meaning to the Self. If I have an infirmity, for example, I choose in which way I shall "exist" that infirmity. I may "exist" it as " 'intolerable,' 'humiliating,' 'to be hidden,' 'to be revealed to all,' 'object of pride,' 'justification of my failures,' etc." [53] The concept of the *pour-soi's* "existing" itself, as we shall see later, is the key to Sartre's theory of the Self and of human freedom. In later sections we shall discuss this concept in great detail. At the present time it is not possible to define the concept any further, since we have not yet exposited those correlated ideas necessary to its comprehension.

---

[51] EN, 389–390. "We have surrendered all claims to endowing ourselves *first* with a body in order *then* to study the way in which we seize or modify the world through it. But, on the contrary, we have given as foundation to the disclosure of the body as such, our original relation to the world, that is, our very arising in the midst of being. Far from the body's being first *for us* and revealing the things to us, it is the things-utensils which, in their original appearance, indicate our body to us."

[52] Sartre uses the verb "to exist" as a transitive verb with a direct object. In other words, he may speak of "I exist myself" (when "I" *bring into existence* "myself") as distinguished from "I myself exist" (when the statement simply means that I myself do exist). It seems impossible to get away from Sartre's use of "to exist." For example, Sartre writes (EN, 418): "*J'existe mon corps*," which can only be translated: "I exist my body."

The seizing of the Self as Self, as pure facticity, as consciousness which does not "exist" itself via pain or other such phenomena—such seizure is the taste of *nausea*. "A discrete and insurmountable nausea perpetually reveals my body to my consciousness." [54] Sartre's novel *Nausea* makes clear that what is grasped in nausea by the *pour-soi* is its stuffness, its *en-soi*. Physical nausea is only one of the manifestations of existential nausea. "Far from our having to understand this term of *nausea* as a metaphor derived from our physiological loathings, it is, on the contrary, on its foundation that are produced all the concrete and empirical nauseas (nausea before rotten food, fresh blood, excrements, etc.) which lead us to vomiting." [55]

The appearance of my body to the Other or vice versa is not the way in which the Other is truly manifested to me or the way in which I am manifested to the Other. This would be a relation of pure exteriority, whereas the real relationship is one of interiority. "My liaison to the Other is inconceivable if it is not an internal relation." [56] The internal relation needed, then, is the "signification" of the body. The signification of the body is defined through the relations which the body has to the chairs it sits on, the sidewalks it walks on, etc. "The body is totality of the significant relations to the world . . . The body could not appear, in fact, without sustaining, with the totality of that which it is, significant relations." [57]

The Other appears to me as related to the totality of "significations" he expresses. Thus, the body of the Other is a certain distance from that glass, in a specific relation to the chair he sits on, etc. I can understand the Being of the body of the Other only by comprehending the Other as he exists within a total situation.[58] The totality referred to here may be explained as follows: an organ or part of another person appears to me in relation to his total situation. If the Other holds his fist directly before my eyes, I do not, therefore, infer that his fist is larger than his body. Here the traditional notion of perspective is translated into the signification-perspective of life. Fists are not simply

[54] EN, 404.
[55] *Ibid.*
[56] *Ibid.*, 405.
[57] *Ibid.*, 411.
[58] *Ibid.*, 412.

objects; they are parts of beings who themselves are parts of situations in which their fists are related to what they are engaged in.[59]

Just as we cannot truly seize the organ of the body apart from the totality, we cannot speak of the emotion, or passion, or expression of a man apart from the activity through which that emotion, passion, or expression is evidenced. The form of evidencing the emotion *is* the emotion:

> "These knittings of the brows, this redness . . . which seem . . . threatening do not *express* the anger, they *are* the anger. But. it is very necessary to understand: in itself a clenched fist is nothing and means nothing. But also we never perceive a *clenched fist*: we perceive a man who, in a certain situation, clenches his fist. This significant act considered in liaison with the past and the "possibles," understood from the synthetic totality 'body-in-situation,' *is* the anger." [60]

Within a specific situation—for example, the relation of the glass to Pierre, who happens to be sitting in *that* armchair—the Other has the freedom to change his situation (Pierre can move to the couch). Because the body of the Other is "seized" only in so far as we must admit the referential quality of the situation of the Other (all references of utensils are to the Other, since they are his utensils), we are compelled to admit the freedom of the Other.

Because of the freedom of the Other, we can never consider his body as mere body; it is always greater than the facticity of the body, since the Other passes beyond, transcends, that facticity in his engagement. There is an objectivity, a mere facticity of the body, but in so far as I grasp the Other in his surroundings, in his engagement, in synthetic totality, I do not observe that facticity.[61]

Three ontological dimensions of the body have been defined in the relations between the Being of the Self and the Being of the Other:

> "I exist my body; such is its first dimension. My body is utilized and known by the Other: such is its second dimension.

---

[59] EN, 413.

[60] *Ibid.*

[61] *Ibid.,* 418. "The body for the Other is the magical object par excellence. Thus the body of the Other is always 'body-more-than-body,' because the Other is given to me without intermediary and totally in the perpetual passing beyond of its facticity."

But in so far as *I am for the Other, the Other* is disclosed to me as the subject for which I am object. It is a question even here, as we have seen, of my fundamental relation with the Other. I exist then for myself as known by the Other by virtue of body. Such is the third ontological dimension of my body." [62]

In the third ontological dimension I know my body as it is for the Other, yet I have a new knowledge of it myself. This new knowledge is gained during certain states of my body: when I perspire in fear of the Other, when I blush, etc. In such instances, I have a consciousness of my body not as it is for me, but as it is for the Other.[63]

The Being which we are escapes us, and we, paradoxically, get to know that Being in tangential fashion through the manner in which we experience that Being as it is for the Other. Thus, for example, we can never know our body as it *is*; only another sees us in totality so that he sees our body as it *is*; but in being aware of the fact that I am object for another who sees my body as it *is*, I feel timidity or shame, and in the experience of that timidity or shame my body becomes known to me as body-known-by-the-Other. "It appears to us then that the Other accomplishes for us a function of which we are incapable, which however is incumbent on us: *to see us as we are.*" [64]

4. ATTITUDES TOWARD THE OTHER

The introduction of the relations of timidity and shame leads Sartre to a consideration of the concrete relations the *pour-soi* has with the Other. The attitudes of the *pour-soi* toward the Other which Sartre describes are Love, Language, Masochism, Indifference, Desire, Sadism, and Hate.

a) Love.—Love presents an ambiguous and paradoxical relationship. In loving the Other, we are faced with the problem of whether such love is love of the Other as object or as subject. Do we necessarily appropriate the Other as object in the love relation? If so, then in what sense is the freedom of the Other maintained? Or is love by necessity a severing and destruction of the freedom of the loved one? Again, what effect do these possibilities have on the lover?

[62] EN, 418–419.
[63] *Ibid.,* 420.
[64] *Ibid.,* 421.

Since, for Sartre, the freedom of the Other is the foundation of my Being, I am in danger of losing my freedom if the freedom of the Other is lost.[65] If I shatter the subjectivity of the Other whom I love by rendering him an object in my world, I am at the same time endangering my own status, my own freedom; for it is always through the Other that my freedom is determined.

Thus, there is a general paradox of love: the lover makes of his loved one an object, and, in so doing, negates the freedom of the loved one. But the freedom of the loved one was what the lover sought in his love. In loving he has destroyed the love he sought. The lover wishes for an impossible thing: "He wishes to possess a freedom as freedom."[66] Since this is in principle impossible, love is a paradoxical relation which results in frustration.

b) Language.—The problem of language is exactly parallel to the problem of the body, and the descriptions which were valid in one case are valid in the other.[67] It is through the Other that we learn the true nature of our body. The Other sees us as we are. Thus, we must turn to the Other to learn what we are, and this is necessarily accomplished through language. Since it is only through the Other that we can see ourselves, we depend upon the description the Other gives us concerning ourselves. These descriptions which we receive through language, then, are the sole way in which we may hope to comprehend ourselves as we exist for the Other.[68]

c) Masochism.—In masochism the desire of the masochist is to be completely and purely an object for the Other. The flight of the masochist is toward *en-soi*. It is the masochist who refuses to be anything more than an object for the Other. In feeling himself an object for the Other, the masochist experiences the feeling of shame, and it is this feeling that he seeks in his abnormality. The masochist wants and loves his shame.[69]

But masochism is also the assumption of guilt. The masochist is guilty from the sole fact that he is an object. He is also guilty in so far

---

[65] EN, 433.
[66] *Ibid.,* 434.
[67] *Ibid.,* 442.
[68] *Ibid.,* 421.
[69] *Ibid.,* 446.

as he willingly allows himself to be made an object for the Other.[70] But the guilt of the masochist is just part of his paradoxical condition, which makes of masochism a necessary failure.

Masochism carries the germ of its destruction within itself, for while the goal of the masochist is to reduce himself to an utter object for some Other's subjectivity, he must, in his masochism, treat that other person, who beats him, whips him, etc., as an object for *his* subjectivity. It is, then, in vain that the masochist permits himself to be mistreated or tortured, since he is mistreated or tortured by the Other, who ultimately is object for him. Thus, the more the masochist attempts to "taste his objectivity, the more he will be submerged by the consciousness of his subjectivity." [71]

d) Indifference.—The attitude of indifference is induced by a "blindness" toward Others. In being indifferent, the *pour-soi* retreats from Others, chooses to ignore reality. The *pour-soi* practices, then, a sort of solipsism of attitude: the Others walking by me in the street are hardly noticed, they are simply "coefficients of adversity," like walls or buildings. . . . "I do not even imagine that they can *look at me*." [72]

Thus, "there are men who die without having suspected—except during brief and terrifying illuminations—what the Other·was." [73]

e) Desire.—"Desire" is always sexual desire, which is "my original attempt to possess the free subjectivity of the Other through its objectivity-for-me." [74] The questions which now arise are: What is desire? *Of what* is there desire? and *What* is it that desires? [75]

Sartre's answer to the first question is that "desire is nothing other than one of the grand forms which the disclosure of the body of the Other can take." [76] He also says that "desire is an attempt to undress the body of its movements as of its clothes and to make it exist as pure flesh; it is an attempt at *incarnation* of the body of the Other." [77] This

[70] EN, 446.
[71] *Ibid.*, 447.
[72] *Ibid.*, 449.
[73] *Ibid.*
[74] *Ibid.*, 451.
[75] *Ibid.*, 455.
[76] *Ibid.*
[77] *Ibid.*, 459.

"incarnation" of the body of the Other is accomplished through the "caress," which Sartre describes as a "shaping" through which I make the flesh of the Other "be born." [78]

Desire, however, also leads to a paradox—an "impossible ideal": "to possess the transcendence of the Other as pure transcendence and yet as *body;* to reduce the Other to his simple *facticity,* because he is then in the midst of my world, but to make this facticity be a perpetual presentation of its 'nihilating' transcendence." [79]

f) Sadism.—Sadism is the correlated reverse of masochism. Like masochism it is destined to failure. "The object of sadism is immediate appropriation. . . . Sadism is, at one and the same time, refusal to be incarnated and flight from all facticity, and effort to become master of the facticity of the Other." [80]

"What the sadist seeks . . . with so much tenacity, what he wants to knead with his hands and break under his fist is the freedom of the Other." [81] To accomplish this the sadist seeks the moment of decision when his victim gives in under the torture. At that moment what the sadist sought for is momentarily gained. The body of his victim "is entirely flesh, panting and obscene, it keeps the position that the torturers have given to it, not that which it would have taken by itself, the cords which bind it sustain it as an inert thing and, by that, it has ceased to be the object which moves spontaneously." [82] This tortured body is the symbol of enslaved freedom.

But there is a necessary cycle of defeat in sadism, and for several reasons. Although the sadist tries to appropriate the transcendent freedom of the Other, "this freedom remains, in principle, out of reach, and the more the sadist is intent on treating the Other as instrument, the more this freedom escapes him." [83] The sadist discovers the failure of his efforts when his victim *looks* at him. In the Look the sadist realizes "that he could not act on the freedom of the Other, even by compelling the Other to humiliate himself and to beg for mercy, for it is precisely in and by the absolute freedom of the Other that a world

---

[78] EN, 459.
[79] *Ibid.,* 463–464.
[80] *Ibid.,* 469.
[81] *Ibid.,* 473.
[82] *Ibid.,* 474.
[83] *Ibid.,* 476.

happens to exist in which there are a sadist and instruments of torture and a hundred pretexts for being humiliated and disowned." [84] The Look is for the sadist more unbearable than crucifixion or death, for it haunts his Being as pure guilt. "The look of the Other in the world of the sadist makes the meaning and the goal of the sadism collapse." [85]

All the conducts of men toward each other are only variations, increased complexes, of the original attitudes of sadism and masochism (and a third—hate). Thus, conducts such as collaboration, obedience, maternal love, pity, and good will are fundamentally founded on masochism and sadism. In the description of such complex attitudes, it is necessary to take into consideration historical situation, concrete particulars, etc.; "but they all enclose within them as their skeleton the sexual relations." [86]

g) *Hate.*—Hatred is the attempt of the Self to avoid being an object for another by wishing the extinction or destruction of the Other. But in order to hate an Other, I must first admit the existence and the subjectivity of the Other. Thus, hate carries with it necessarily a recognition of the freedom of the Other.

"The occasion which provokes hate is simply the act of the Other by which I have been placed in a state of submitting to his freedom." [87] But in hating the Other, who has appropriated me, and in recognizing his freedom, I am hating all Others as well. My hatred for the Other is symbolic, then, of my hatred for all Others.[88]

But this hatred is necessarily involved in a failure, for even if I succeed in overcoming the Other, the very attempt I make to triumph over him is admittance of the fact that he existed. I am unable to prevent myself from recognizing the existence of the Other, even though that existence may be part of my past. Thus, once I have been made an object for the Other, I am "contaminated" in my Being for the rest of my days, "even if the Other has been entirely overcome." [89]

---

[84] EN, 476.
[85] *Ibid.,* 477.
[86] *Ibid.*
[87] *Ibid,* 482.
[88] *Ibid.,* 483.
[89] *Ibid.*

5. BEING WITH (MIT-SEIN)

The investigation of the Other leads to the concept of Being-With: the 'we.' The problem of Being-With is one of the communal relations of the Self with the Other and with Others. The experience of the 'we' is a true experience, according to Sartre, for "the very existence and use of this grammatical form (we) refers back necessarily to a real experience of the *'Mit-sein'*." [90] However, this experience of the *'Mit-sein'* is a psychological, not an ontological structure.

The rejection of the *Mit-sein* as an ontological structure is a fundamental concept of EN. For Sartre, human reality is not originally communal but, rather, is in conflict—in necessary and perpetual conflict. Thus, "the essence of the rapports between consciousnesses is not the *'mit-sein,'* it is conflict."[91]

The concept of action is implicit in the philosophy of Sartre. In its dialectical flight, in its relation toward Others, the *pour-soi acts.* It is now necessary, Sartre says, to raise such questions as: What does it mean to act? Why does the *pour-soi* act? How can the *pour-soi* act? The foundation for the answers to these questions has been constructed already in Sartre's considerations of nihilation, facticity, the body, the Other, and, of course, the *pour-soi* and the *en-soi.*[92] Through a new interrogation of these concepts, Sartre proposes to reveal the ontological nature of action and to show the relation of action to man's freedom.

[90] EN, 484.
[91] *Ibid.,* 502.
[92] *Ibid.,* 503.

Chapter III

THE SELF

1. FREEDOM

According to Sartre, every action is, in principle, intentional; and true action implies a consciousness of acting on the part of the actor. Thus, if someone throws away a lighted cigarette which happens to set off a fuse, which in turn produces an explosion, he has not *acted*. On the other hand, true action *has* been taken by the worker whose job it is to follow out the steps required to set off a dynamite charge.[1] Since action is necessarily intentional, no political or economic fact can cause action in the individual. Motivation is inner.[2]

The "indispensible and fundamental condition of all action is the freedom of the acting Being." [3] Freedom is evidenced in the *pour-soi* in so far as the *pour-soi* exists as "lack." The "lack" of the *pour-soi* is its Nothingness. Because the *pour-soi* "exists" itself through flight, it *is* nothing, for its existence is always non-static: the *pour-soi* is not that which it is and is that which it is not.[4]

Choice, freedom, and action are inextricably bound together in the existence of the *pour-soi*. There can be no freedom if there is no choice; there can be no choice if there is no freedom; there can be no action where there is no freedom. "Freedom, choice, nihilation, temporalization are but one sole and selfsame thing." [5]

Sartre means something quite different by 'freedom' than is intended in common usage or in general philosophical usage. Freedom, as it is generally understood, might be defined as "the ability to satisfy needs plus the ability to develop new needs, with the understanding,

---

[1] EN, 508.
[2] *Ibid.*, 510–511.
[3] *Ibid.*, 511.
[4] *Ibid.*, 558.
[5] *Ibid.*, 543.